THE RABBEANS: A TRIBAL SOCIETY ON THE EUPHRATES FROM YAḪDUN-LIM TO JULIUS CAESAR

by
Michael C. Astour
Southern Illinois University at Edwardsville

This article deals with the West Semitic nomadic tribe of the Rabbeans, who at the time of the Mari archives belonged to the Benjaminite confederation and controlled one of the mixed urban-tribal states on the upper Middle Euphrates. It traces the history of the tribe to the end of the Late Bronze and examins its role in the struggle of the contemporaneous great powers. Then, after a long historical gap, it shows the descendants of the Rabbeans re-emerge, under the same name, in the same area, and in a very similar political role, during the struggle for Syria in the first century B.C.

The earliest mention of the Rabbû tribe[1] appears in the great foundation inscription of Yaḫdun-Lim, son of Yaggid-Lim, king of Mari about 1750 (low chronology).[2] He started the consolidation of his state by defeating and subduing the nomadic and seminomadic tribes of the Middle Euphrates region who belonged to the West Semitic ethnic group of Ḫaneans.[3] He assumed the title of "king of Mari and of the land of Ḫana,"[4] a characteristic expression of the dual, urban-tribal, nature of his kingdom,[5] one of several states of that type which arose about that same time in Mesopotamia and Syria, and some of which we shall meet presently. He then undertook an expedition to the Mediterranean Sea in order to cut timber in the coastal mountains.[6] To reach them, he had to traverse the region of Ḫalab, which at that very time was expanding into a powerful kingdom under the tribal name of Yamḫad.[7] The people of that area were evidently taken by surprise and offered no resistance. But Sumu-epuḫ, the ruler of Yamḫad, riposted by organizing against Yaḫdun-Lim a rebellion on the Middle Euphrates.

After reporting his success in the Cedar and Boxwood mountains, Yaḫdun-Lim's relation continues: "In that same year the following kings rebelled against him: La'ûm, king of Samanum and of the land of Ubrabûm;[8] Baḫlu-kulim, king of Tuttul and of the land of Amnanûm; Ayālum, king of Abattum and of the land of Rabbûm. An army of Sumu-epuḫ from the land of Yamḫad came to their help. In the city of Samanum they all gathered against him, the league of the Benjaminites,[9] (but) he defeated these three kings of the Benjaminites in a great battle. He routed their army and the army that had come to their help, made a massacre (among them)."[10] This passage informs us about three more urban-tribal states similar in essence to the dual kingdom of Mari (an ancient Akkadian-speaking city) and the land of the Ḫanean tribesmen. They were located upstream from Mari, and their enumeration proceeds from southeast to northwest.

The city of Samanum, as we learn from other Mari documents, belonged later on, after its annexation to Mari, to the administrative district of Terqa.[11] The Benjaminite tribe of Ubrabûm occupied the left bank of the Euphrates opposite their Rabbean kinsmen.[12] This places La'ûm's kingdom in the area between the lower Balīḫ and the lower Ḫabūr.

The second of the allied kingdoms combined the ancient, important city of Tuttul with the territory of another Benjaminite tribe, Amnanûm (or Awnanûm), part of which had established a dual kingdom of the same type far to the southeast, around the historic city of Uruk.[13] The general position of the northern Amnanûm state is determined by the location of its capital, Tuttul, which has now been definitively identified with the enormous Tell Biyāʿ near the western bank of the Baliḫ just above its confluence with the Euphrates.[14] The land of the Amnanûm extended therefore from the lower reaches of the Baliḫ westwards along the left bank of the Euphrates, perhaps as far as its great bend. This state, like the preceding, was incorporated by Yaḫdun-Lim into the royal domain of Mari, and remained so under his successors. This annexation was reflected in Yaḫdun-Lim's new title: "King of Mari, Tuttul, and the land of Ḫana."[15]

The third state, that of the Rabbûm tribe, was located on the Syrian bank of the Euphrates, facing the lands of the Amnanûm and Ubrabûm. Its western boundary passed below the important river port Emar (called Imar in the Mari records) which, at the time of Yaḫdun-Lim, formed a separate state.[16] The identification of Emar with Old Meskeneh (Bālis)[17] has been brilliantly confirmed by the recent excavations of that site.[18] A natural border between Emar and the land of the Rabbeans is provided by the broad spur of limestone hills which sharply separates the plain of Meskeneh from the plain of Dibsī. In the southeast, the territory of Rabbûm probably reached the Ǧebel Bišri, though some parts of the tribe, as this is usual with nomads, lived much farther downstream.[19] Unlike the two previously mentioned states, the kingdom of Rabbûm was not annexed to Mari. It remained a self-governing political entity, technically within the zone of influence of Yamḫad,[20] but, as we shall see, allied with Mari during the Assyrian interregnum.

The location of Abattum, the capital of the Rabbûm state, can be established from the following data. The territory of the Rabbeans was adjacent to the Mariote district of Tuttul and was separated from it by the Euphrates. According to ARM IV 6, it was the governor of Tuttul who was instructed to send boats for ferrying the Rabbeans (*Ra-ab-ba-yu*) from the Yamḫadian to the Mariote bank.[21] Their capital must have been located on the same (right) bank of the Euphrates.[22] It appears indeed in both versions of the Old Babylonian itinerary of a round-trip Larsa-Emar[23] as a station between Tuttul and Emar. Since the former city lay on the left bank, and the latter on the right bank of the Euphrates, the caravan had to cross the river, and the easiest spot for doing it has always been Raqqah, the classical Nicephorium, 4 km. south of Tuttul, and very probably the site of that city's harbor.[24] The distance between Tuttul and Abattum could be covered in one stage (Urbana Itinarary), or in two stages, with a stop designated simply "bank of the Euphrates" (Yale Itinerary). This indicates that the distance between these two cities was greater than the average length of a day's march in the Urbana and Yale Itineraries, i.e., 27 km.[25] At a distance of *ca.* 34 km. (by road) from Tuttul (Tell Biyāʾ) rises the double cone of Tell Ṯadeyyēn ("Two Breasts").[26] According to E. Herzfeld, its height is 40 m. over the river, 30 m. over the plain; it is partially a natural hillock, but its upper levels consist of settlement debris. Herzfeld found that all of the few pottery fragments picked up on its surface were "very old, pre-Islamic and even pre-classical"; he attributed them to what he called "Babylonian times."[27] Ṯell Tadyyēn stands over a ford, the land around it is quite productive, and the location offers good conditions for settlement (which is not common along that segment of the Euphrates); this is evidenced by the presence, directly west of the tell, of extensive ruins of some later town.[28] On the basis of these concurrent indications, we can safely identify Abattum with Tell Ṯadyyēn.[29]

The Rabbean country, as we can gather from the correspondence of Šamši-Adad I and his sons, was, for all intents and purposes, independent from both the neighboring Yamḫad and the Assyrian régime at Mari. The Rabbeans were allied with Yasmaḫ-Addu, the Assyrian regent of Mari and the western part of Šamši-Adad's empire, and sometimes moved, with official Mariote assistance, to the left bank of the Euphrates, no doubt in search of pastures.[30] But they were very jealous of their traditional freedoms, and were strongly opposed to census taking, regarded by Bedouins as a sign of submission, even if it affected not them but their Benjaminite "brothers" on the Mariote side of the river.[31] When Šamši-Adad tried to organize a grand coalition against Sumu-epuḫ of Yamḫad by mustering against him his northern vassals, the "men" (rulers) of Ḫaššum, Uršum, and Carchemish, he also took care to assure

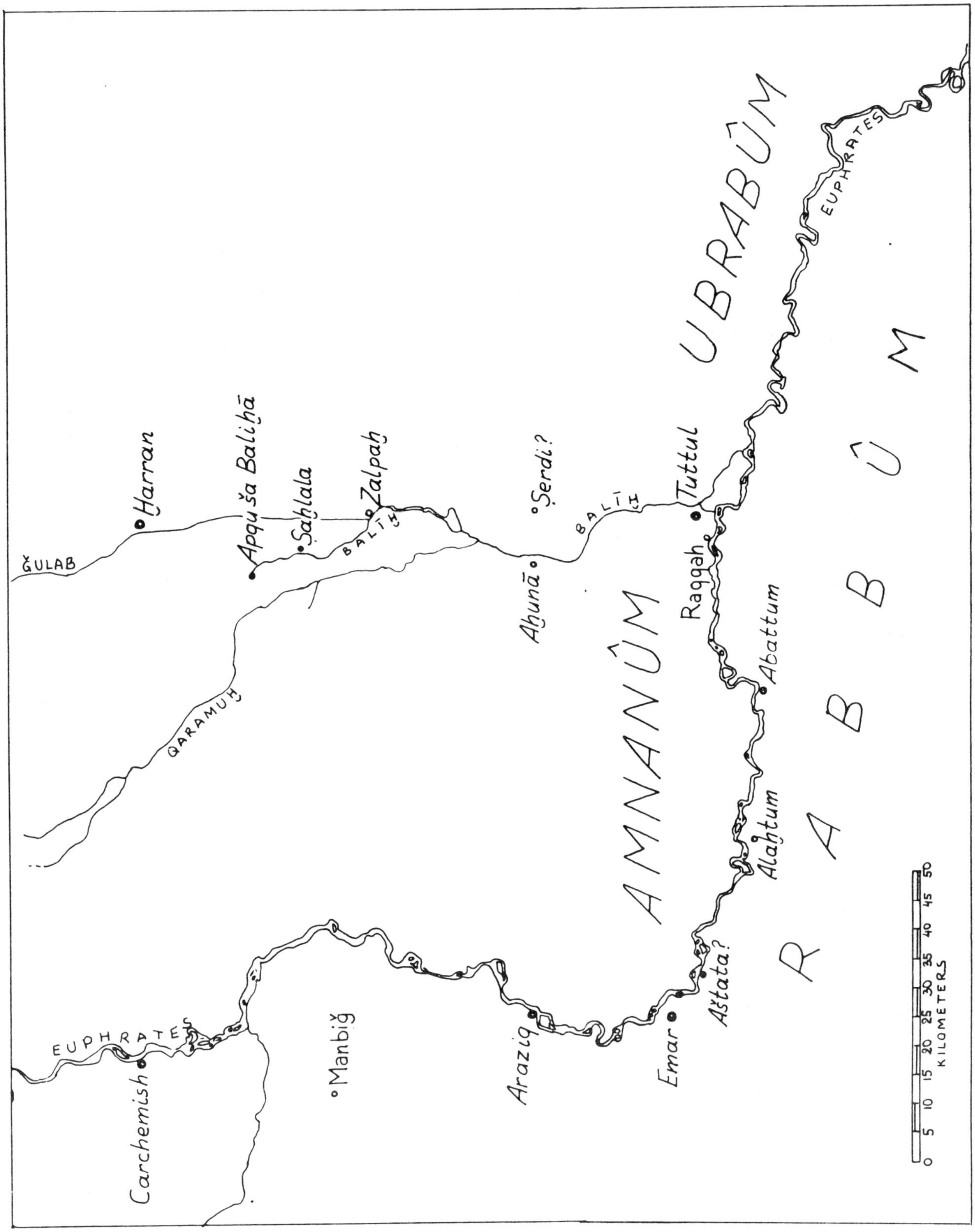
Harran
Apqu ša Baliḫā
Saḫlala
Zalpaḫ
Ṣerdi?
Tuttul
ǦULAB
BALĪḪ
Aḫunā
Raqqah
Abattum
QARAMUḪ
AMNANÛM
UBRABÛM
RABBÛM
Alaḫtum
Aštata?
Emar
Arazig
Manbiǧ
EUPHRATES
Carchemish
0 5 10 15 20 25 30 35 40 45 50
KILOMETERS

Figure 1. Map.

the cooperation of the "man" of the Rabbeans (LÚ *Ra-ab-ba-[yu]*).[32] One perceives that the Rabbeans, owing to the strategic position of their territory at the confines of Syria and Mesopotamia, on the important Euphrates road, tried to play independent politics between rival great powers–a situation that was to recur more than once in subsequent periods.

After the end of the Assyrian régime in Mari, an administrative text records the payment of *3* GÍN KU. BABBAR *Sà*! *-am-sà-nu* 3 GÍN *Na-ap-sú-um* GAL [. . . . . .] *2* LÚ.MEŠ *Su-tu-ú* DU[MU].MEŠ *ši-[ip]-ri š[a R]a-b[i-i]m* "3 shekels of silver to Samsanu, 3 shekels to Napsum, chief [. . . . . . .], two Sutû-men, messengers of the Rabbeans."[33] Another text lists 5 GÍN *Ra-bi-ú-um Su-tu-ú*.[34] These passages are of considerable interest as testimonies of some kind of autonomy of the Rabbeans at the time of Zimri-Lim, and as an indication that the Rabbeans were reckoned at Mari as Sutû, a common term for Bedouins of the Syrian desert.[35] However, a process of sedentarization began to take place among some Rabbean groups. A settlement in the Terqa or Mari district of the kingdom of Mari was called *Za-ar-ri Ra-bi-yu-um* ki,[36] to be compared to *Za-ar-ri*ki *Aw-na-an* ki,[37] in the same area, named for a splinter of another Benjaminite tribe. Part of the Rabbean clan of Bīt-Awin[38] was established, at the time of Zimri-Lim, in the town of Appān, near Mari, while the other part continued a nomadic way of life as a "steppe clan" (*ḫibrūm ša nawīm*); but the clan as a whole owned the lands under cultivation.[39]

The same phenomenon is observable in the Rabbean country proper. As far downstream as Abū Nureyrah (31 km. from Old Meskeneh-Emar), "a fertile belt 1 to 3 miles wide can produce wheat and barley without irrigation."[40] A Mari letter which speaks of Zarri-Awnan, of the Ubrabû tribe, and of Benjaminites in general, mentions that a certain Dadi-Ḫadun was threshing his grain at Abattum.[41] Another letter tells that "the banks of the Euphrates are in a state of alert: boys and girls, as well as grain, are gathered together," and the Benjaminites are restoring Abattum.[42] Thus, while the majority of the Rabbeans remained nomadic, some of their land along the Euphrates was under cultivation. How large was the tribe? By way of analogy, one may recall that in 1915, when there was no agriculture whatever in that area, the Euphrates Valley below Meskeneh was the preserve of a subdivision of the Beduoin Šabʿan tribe, which counted eighteen clans and 3,000 tents or family units.[43]

Toward the end of Zimri-Lim's rule, a town of the Rabbean country became an object of contest between Mari and Yamḫad. In addition to the entire left bank of the Euphrates, Mari possessed on its right bank the town of Alaḫtum, which was a river port with considerable storage facilities[44] and probably served as a custom house.[45] Its location can be deduced from the Urbana Itinerary which places *[A-l]a-at-tu-u[m]*[46] at two stages west of Abattum, while the Yale Itinerary divides the segment Abattum–Emar into four stages;[47] this puts the site of Alattum approximately halfway between Tell Ṯedeyyēn and Old Meskeneh. The only spot in that general area which provides conditions for a permanent urban settlement is Banāt Abū Hureyrah, the former site of the Roman Sephe, the medieval Arab Ṣiffīn,[48] some 37 km. from Old Meskeneh and 30 km. from Tell Ṯedeyyēn.[49] The prophets of the shrines of Adad at Ḫalab and Kallasu, acting on behalf of the king of Yamḫad, insisted that Zimri-Lim, whom Adad had restored on his ancestral throne, turn over Alaḫtum to Adad as his inheritance, i.e., transfer it to Yamḫad.[50] But Zimri-Lim, who had no intention of doing this, had his own prophets to counter the claims of the other side. One of them announced in the name of the goddess Diritum that *a-na Zi-im-r[i-Li-im] A-la-i-tum na-ad-[na-at]* "To Zimri-Lim Alaʾitum has been given."[51] J. Sasson had the excellent idea of seeing a toponym in the hitherto unexplained *a-la-i-tum*[52] and of identifying it with Alaḫtum as "another case in the *dossier* of Mari-Yamḫad split."[53]

In the event, when Ḫammurapi of Babylon turned against his former ally Zimri-Lim and subdued his kingdom, Yamḫad did not interfere on behalf of Mari and profited from its downfall by annexing some territory between the Euphrates and the Balīḫ.[54] The tribal state of the Rabbeans must have also passed under the sovereignty of Yamḫad, and, in all probability, its people resented it. The government of Mari had collected custom duties from all ships sailing past its checkpoint on the Euphrates,[55] which, as it seems, was located within the Rabbean territory. One may plausibly surmise that the Rabbeans were very much interested in taking over the lucrative control of the commercial traffic on and along the Euphrates. If Yamḫad, as one should expect, tried to prevent the Rabbeans from imposing tolls on its ships and caravans, this in itself was sufficient for causing serious frictions between the two sides. In addition to it, there was the permanent antagonism between Bedouins and settled populations.

These general considerations help us to understand why in the critical time of Yamḫad's struggle for its very existence against the repeated onslaughts of the Hittites in the sixteenth century, the attackers found a willing ally in Aštata, by which name the state of the Rabbeans was known at that time. The location of the land of Aštata is established by a passage in the treaty between Šuppiluliumaš of Hatti and Šattiwaza of Mitanni.[56] It occupied the right bank of the Euphrates "across the river from Mitanni" (*e-bi-ir-ti ša* KUR ^{uru}*Mi-it-ta-an-ni*) and, at least in the fourteenth century, some territory on the left bank, including the town of Aḫuna on the lower Baliḫ.[57] It did not comprise Emar which, under the Hittite Empire, continued as a separate state.[58] It seems that the city of Aštata[59] had by then replaced Abattum as the capital of the Rabbeans (we shall see that their tribal name persisted till at least the end of the Late Bronze Age). The exact location of that city is, so far, unknown.[60]

The role of Aštata in the first Hittite conquest of Northern Syria emerges from the historical preamble to the treaty between Muršiliš II, Great King of Hatti, and his nephew Talmi-Šarruma, the second king of the Hittite appanage of Ḫalab.[61] We follow H. Otten in assuming that all mentions in this preamble of the royal name *Ḫattušiliš* refer to the first king of that name, the founder of the Hittite Old Kingdom, and not, in part, to an otherwise unattested king Ḫattušiliš II who supposedly ruled in the middle of the fifteenth century.[62] According to the preamble, Ḫattušiliš "completed" the "great kingship" previously held by Ḫalab, i.e., put an end to its status of an independent kingdom, and transferred some towns and border areas of the land of Ḫalab (the royal domain of Yamḫad) and of the land of Nuḫašše (the south-eastern territories of Yamḫad)[63] to "the people of the land of Aštati." However, the king of Ḫalab soon broke his (imposed) oath of allegiance to Ḫattušiliš and turned to the king of the great North Mesopotamian state, intermittently called Ḫanigalbat and Mitanni in the preamble, who came to his assistance and returned to the "people of the land of Ḫalab" and to the "people of the land of Nuḫašši" the towns and border areas previously lost to Aštata.

It is evident that Aštata, which was rewarded by Ḫattušiliš with towns and territories at the expense of Ḫalab and Nuḫašše, was an ally of the Hittites against Yamḫad and Mitanni. The interests of those two states, which controlled, respectively, the areas west and east of the Euphrates, were certainly opposed to the exploitation of the Euphrates route by the Rabbeans, and both must have restricted, to the best of their ability, their encroachments. No wonder that the Rabbeans of Aštata joined the Hittites, who fought both Yamḫad and Mitanni, as soon as they appeared on their horizon. The Hittite attack on Yamḫad from the north gave the Rabbeans the opportunity to raid it from the east. It is very probable that the towns in Ḫalab and Nuḫašše, which were granted to them by Ḫattušiliš, had already been sacked and seized by them. In our opinion, it was these Bedouin raids, and not any hypothetical changes of climate,[64] that were responsible for the destructions and decline of population in the areas of Northern Syria bordering on the desert which took place in the transition period between Middle and Late Bronze Ages.[65]

It seems that the alliance between Aštata and the Hittites lasted throughout the whole period of the Old Kingdom's Syrian wars. An allusion to it can perhaps be found in a very damaged fragment of an Old Hittite historical narrative (KUB XL 4),[66] which tells of military operations in Syria and mentions the well-known city of Uršu,[67] the hitherto unattested city of Giala, Yarim-Lim son of Piazzi who was the "man" of Ebla,[68] and a certain Atraduš (Hittianization of *Atar-Addu* or *Atri-Addu*),[69] who made peace with the (Hittite) king and, apparently, led his troops and chariots against Yarim-Lim, the ruler of Emar and probably a member of the royal house of Yamḫad.[70] This Atraduš may well have been the ruler of Emar's neighbor, Aštata. The strategic location of Aštata must also be taken into account in considering Muršiliš I daring march on Babylon in 1531. It had already been noted that the expedition may have been preceded and facilitated by an alliance between the Hittites and the Kassites who at that time controlled the kingdom of Ḫana on the Middle Euphrates.[71] But before reaching Ḫana one had to cross the whole length of Aštata, and here its pre-Hittite orientation was crucial. A few years later, Hantiliš undertook an expedition to Aštata, [. . . . . . .]iya, Ḫurpana, and Carchemish;[72] the order of enumeration and the sequence of the narrative seem to indicate that the expedition aimed at assisting the loyal but distant ally, Aštata, against the Hurrians (Mitanni), but without success.

We do not know the political status of Aštata in the period of Mitannian supremacy. The two mentions of ^{uru}*Aš-ta-te* in Alalaḫ texts of Level IV[73] do not help us. Then, after Šuppiluliumaš's Second Syrian War,[74] as we learn from that king's aforementioned treaty with Šattiwaza, Aštata was included into the new Hittite appanage kingdom of Carchemish.[75] But how was it administered? The recently discovered Meskeneh texts revealed that Emar, though well within the limits of the appanage, preserved nevertheless its old royal dynasty under the suzerainty of the kings of Carchemish.[76] The same was probably true for Aštata. At any rate, it was well integrated in the Hittite imperial structure. Muršiliš II used it as a base during the insurrection of Nuḫašše and Kinza.[77] Its cults and festivals were known and recorded as far as Ḫattušaš.[78] Aštata also appears in a text from Meskeneh[79] in a context which, according to the publisher, suggests that it belonged to the kingdom of Emar, or rather, one may surmise, that it was, along with Emar, under the jurisdiction of Carchemish. It is extremely interesting that other Meskeneh tablets mention, in a similar context, the tribal name of the Rabbeans in the forms *Ra-ab-ba, Ra-ab-ba-an,* or *Ra-bi-*[*i*].[80] Was it used in the thirteenth century to designate a tribal district or a town, and, in the latter event, was that town identical with the ancient capital of the Rabbeans, Abattum?

The Euphrates route, which linked Hittite Syria with friendly Babylonia, remained an important but dangerous road. A passage in the lengthy letter from Ḫattušiliš III to Kadašman-Enlil II tells us that the messenger service between the two countries was often interrupted by Arameans (*Aḫlamû*), and that the Hittite king was ready to provide Babylonian messengers with military escort as soon as they reached Tuttul.[81] Another letter from Ḫattušiliš III, usually thought to have been written to an Assyrian king, but more probably to Kadašman-Turgu of Babylonia,[82] deals with depredations of the (caravans?) of the addressee and of the Hittite land of Carchemish by the people of the city of Turira. Its international status between the zones of sovereignty of Ḫatti on the one hand, of Ḫanigalbat on the other, was unclear, and neither ruler wanted to assume responsibility for its actions. It is likely that Turira was located east of the lower Balīḫ and was a Bedouin stronghold for storing loot.[83] If the powerful Hittite Empire could not entirely restrain the Bedouins along the Euphrates, its fall under the blows of the Peoples of the Sea unleashed a new wave of Bedouin violence. The city of Emar was destroyed in 1187,[84] no doubt by its unruly nomadic neighbors. It had managed to maintain economic relations with Babylonia till its very last moment.

Around 1100, the records of Tiglath-Pileser I depict the right bank of the Euphrates from the confines of the kingdom of Carchemish to the land of Suḫi as infested with Aramean (*Aḫlamû*) tribes, against whom the Assyrian king had to wage no less than fourteen campaigns.[85] But he does not mention the names of individual tribes, and it remains unknown which of the tribal units subsumed under the umbrella designation *Aḫlamû* had lived in that area for many centuries.[86] After this, a deep darkness envelops the valley of the Euphrates from its great bend and almost to the confluence of the Ḫabūr, to last a full millennium. The New Assyrian Empire showed little interest in that segment and hardly controlled it at all.[87] Nor did it play any noticeable role in the road system of the Persian Empire; the commonly accepted location there (at Dibsī or Tell Ṭadeyyēn) of the river crossing at Thapsacus is unfounded and improbable.[88] The Seleucid and Parthian road form Syria to Babylonia avoided the great bend of the Euphrates altogether and followed its left bank between the confluences of the Ḫabūr and the Baliḫ.[89] We notice, however, that from the beginning of the Neo-Assyrian period on, the Arameans of the Syrian Desert have been replaced or absorbed by Arab tribes.

Finally, a vivid and salient picture of the situation on the Middle Euphrates emerges in the first century B.C. It was a time when the Seleucid power in Syria had disintegrated, when Arab chieftains were establishing independent principalities on the country's desert fringe and even deep inland, and when Syria and Northern Mesopotamia were objects of contention between great powers: Armenia, Parthia, and Rome and between opposing Roman factions. The politico-geographical situation in and around Syria of the first century B.C. was quite similar to that of the critical periods of Syrian history in the second millennium, and the information provided by Strabo and Cassius Dio on the Arab tribes along the Euphrates in the later period is of considerable interest for our better understanding, by analogy, the earlier role of Rabbû-Aštata.

At the time of Strabo, the region along the Middle Euphrates was called Parapotamia and belonged to Ara *phylarchoi* "tribal rulers."[90] These chieftains "are each invested with their own particular domains and extract a tribute of no moderate amount" from merchants traveling from Syria to Babylonia.[91] These heavy tolls and lack of security caused most merchants to abandon the direct Euphrates route and to use instead the much longer road across North Mesopotamia and down the Tigris.[92] "The parts this side of the river," says Strabo, "are held by the Romans and by the chieftains of the Arabians as far as Babyloni: some of these chieftains preferring to give ear to the Parthians and others to the Romans, to whom they are neighbors."[93] Or they could change sides and play one side against the other, as this is illustrated by the actions of one of them, called Alchaudonius by Cassius Dio and Alchaedamnus by Strabo. His domai on the right side of the Euphrates, near Osrhoëne and not too far from Apamene, largely coincided with the former territory of the Rabbeans and Aštata. He had no reason to like the short-lived rule over Syria and North Mesopotamia by Tigranes the Great of Armenia, who tried to re-establish law and order in his new domains and forcibly resettled several Arab tribes in the Amanus region.[94] He was thus among the first to come to terms with Lucullus, when the Roman general defeated Tigranes and invaded North Mesopotamia in 69. But the Roman rule did not satisfy him either: in 54, he deserted Crassus and joined the Parthians; ten years later, he led his archers to Apamea on the Orontes to support the Pompeian Caecilius Bassus against the Caesarians.[95] Strabo, reporting this episode, adds a very significant detail: "Among the allies of Bassus was also Alchaedamnus, king of the Rhambaeans, who were nomads this side of the Euphrates River;[96] and he was a friend of the Romans, but upon the belief that he was being treated unjustly by the Roman governors he retired to Mesopotamia and then went into the service of Bassus as a mercenary."[97]

These nomadic *Rhambaioi* completely correspond—with regard to both their territory and their ethnic name—to the Rabbeans of the second millennium. The shift of a geminated *b* into *mb* is not uncommon in Greek transcriptions of Semitic names; in the very same chapter of Strabo, for instance, the name of another Arab chieftain in Syria is written *Gambaros,* for *gabbār(ā)* "hero," while Pliny called his somewhat later namesake *Gabbaras.*[98] In Old Syriac, indeed, the word *gabbārā* appears as *ganbārā*; the dissimilation of *bb* to *mb, nb* is widespread in all Aramaic dialects.[99] The persistence of this appellation through the Amorite, Aramaic, and Arabic stages of North Syrian linguistic history is no more surprising than the survival, since the Mari Age or earlier, of such toponyms of the Syrian Desert as Tadmor, Nazala, or Bišri despite the constant change of populations in control of these places. We have seen that at the end of the Late Bronze Age the ethnonym *Rabbû* acquired a toponymic meaning; it was taken over, one must conclude, first by the Arameans and then by the Arabs as they moved in and assimilated the previous inhabitants of the territory in question. It was not only the name that remained unchanged from the Mari Age into the incipient Roman epoch: so was also the peculiar function of the tribe which bore it. The easiness with which the Rhambeans migrated across the Euphrates and back recalls us their predecessors and namesakes, the Rabbeans, at the time of Šamši-Adad I. The position of the Rhambeans between the Armenians and the Romans, the Romans and the Parthians, the Pompeians and the Caesarians, was basically the same as that of the Rabbeans of Abattum and Aštata between the Old Assyrian Empire and Yamḫad, Yamhad and Mari, Mitanni and Ḫatti. The exploitation of the Euphrates road by the Rhambeans and other riparian tribes has not changed since the second millennium. The deep raid of the Rhambeans into Northern Syria, all the way to Apamea, in search of mercenary wages and, no doubt, of loot, is not much different from the activities of the people of Aštata at the time of Ḫattušiliš I. What is known about the Rabbeans-Rhambeans from their earliest to their latest appearance in written records

–a span of seventeen hundred years–is a good illustration of a recurring basic pattern in the perennial antagonism between the Desert and the Sown when it becomes intertwined with a struggle of outside powers for the possession of Syria.

NOTES

1. *Ma-at Ra-ab-bi-im* Inscr. Yaḫdun-Lim III:9 (see n. 2); *Ra-ab-bi-i*, G. Dossin, "Benjaminites dans les textes de Mari," *Mélanges syriens offerts à M. René Dussaud*, Paris 1939, 985. Other occurrences and spellings will be quoted further on. The etymology proposed by W. F. Albright, *Yahweh and the Gods of Canaan*, London 1968, 94 n. 140, seems convincing: ". . . *rabbāyū* . . . means transparently 'archer(s)', and is a form . . . from the North-west Semitic stem *rby*, 'to shoot an arrow'." Prof. J. Bottéro, who read the typescript of this article, noted that in an Ur III text from Drehem (C. E. Keiser, BIN III, pl. XVI, No. 139:obv. 3) one may read either ÉRÍN *Ra-bi*[ki] or, less probably, ÉRÍN *Ra-pi₅-qi*. If the first reading is preferred, we believe that the town in question was located in Elam (cf. n. 87, end).
2. G. Dossin, "L'inscription de fondation de Iaḫdun-Lim, roi de Mari," *Syria* 32 (1955) 1-28. Other translations: A. L. Oppenheim *ap. ANET*, 556-57; E. Sollberger et J.-R. Kupper, *Inscriptions royales sumériennes et akkadiennes*, Paris 1971, 145-49; the part on the expedition to the sea translated and discussed by A. Malamat, "Campaigns to the Mediterranean by Iahdunlim and Other Early Mesopotamian Rulers," *ap. Studies in Honor of Benno Landsberger* (*Ass. St.* 16), Chicago 1965, 365-70.
3. On the Ḫaneans see, in the first place, J.-R. Kupper, *Les nomades en Mêsopotamie au temps des rois de Mari*, Paris 1957, 1-46.
4. Inscr. Yaḫdun-Lim I:19.
5. Cf. also the words of Baḫdi-Lim, prefect of the palace of Mari, to King Zimri-Lim: "If thou art king of the Ḫaneans, thou art also king of Akkadians" (ARM VI 76:20-21), i.e., of the Akkadian-speaking, non-tribal population of Mari and other major cities of the kingdom.
6. He speaks of the Cedar Mountain (= Amanus) and the Boxwood Mountain (= Ǧebel Quṣeyr south of Antakya).
7. The use of the term *Yamḫad* in documents of the Old Babylonian period indicates that it was not the name of a territorial district but an ethnonym of the *yaqtal* pattern used as an overall designation of the whole political complex under the sovereignty of the tribal dynasty.
8. Or, *Uprapûm*.
9. *Um-ma-at* DUMU *Mi-im* (III:17). *Ummatum* (a West Semitism) is a cognate of Heb. *ʾummāh* "nation" (cf. A. Malamat, "Mari and the Bible," *JAOS* 82 [1962] 144) and Arabic *ummah* "community" (cf. F. M. Denny, "*Ummah* in the Constitution of Medina," *JNES* 36 [1977] 39-47). The term has a supertribal connotation here and III:28-29: *um-ma-at Ḫa-na ša a-bu-ú Ḫa-na ka-lu-šu-nu* "the Ḫanean *ummatum* of all the Ḫanean sheiks." That DUMU *Mi-im* refers to Benjaminites follows from the frequently occurring Mariote date formula, "The year when Zimri-Lim defeated the Benjaminites," in which the ethnonym is variously written DUMU.MEŠ *Ia-mi-na* / *Ia-mi-ni* / *Ia-mi-nim* / *Ia-mi-im* / *Ia-mi* / *Mi-i* / *Mi-e* (M. Birot, *ARMT* XII, 34 n. 1), and once *ma-ar Mi-i* (ARM XI 43:20, cr. M. L. Burke, *ARMT* XI, 124). We use the conventional form "Benjaminite" rather than "Yaminites" because the spelled-out variant *ma-ar Mi-i* shows that the element DUMU(.MEŠ) "son(s)" was not a mute semantic indicator (as believed by I. J. Gelb, "The Early History of the West Semitic Peoples," *JCS* 15 [1969] 37-38) but was indeed pronounced *mār(ē)* in Akkadian and, doubtless, *bin(ī)* in that people's own West Semitic speech (despite the claim to the contrary by H. Tadmor, "Historical Implications of the Correct Rendering of Akkadian *dâku*," *JNES* 17 [1958] 130 n. 2, on which see H. Cazelles, "Mari et l'Ancien Testament," *ap. XVe Rencontre Assyriologique Internationale*, Paris 1967, 77-78, and A. Malamat, "Aspects of Tribal Societies in Mari and Israel," *ibid.*, 137 n. 1., see also M. Weippert, *The Settlement of the Israelite Tribes in Palestine*, London 1971, 111-12, 123 n. 94.
10. Inscr. Yaḫdun-Lim III:3-23.
11. A. Finet, *ARMT* XV, 133.
12. G. Dossin, "Benjaminites," 985.
13. Sin-kāšid, *ca.* 1800, called himself lugal unug[ki], ga lugal *Am-na-num*: cf. J.-R. Kupper, *Nomades*, 51 and n. 1; A. Falkenstein, "Zu den Inschriften der Grabung in Uruk-Warka 1960-1961," *Baghdader Mitteilungen* 2 (1963) 22-23, 34, 38, 56-64.
14. G. Dossin, "Le site de Tuttul-sur-Balîḫ," *RA* 68 (1974) 25-34.

15. Foundation inscription published by F. Thureau-Dangin, "Iaḫdunlim, roi de Ḫana," *RA* 33 (1936) 49-54, line 5; recent translation: E. Sollberger et J.-R. Kupper, *Inscr. royales*, 244-45.

16. As seen from the date formula MU *Ia-aḫ-du-Li-im da-aw-da-am ša I-ma-ar*^{ki} *i-du-ku-ú* "The year when Iaḫdun-Lim defeated Emar," G. Dossin, "Les noms d'années et d'éponymes dans les 'Archives de Mari'," *ap. Studia Mariana*, Leiden 1950, 52, No. 5.

17. As advocated by G. Dossin, "Une lettre de Zimri-Lim à Iarim-Lim, roi d'Alep," *ap. Proceedings of the Twenty-Third International Congress of Orientalists*, London [1956], 122-23; *idem*, "Le site de la ville de Kahat," *AAS* 11-12 (1961-62) 199.

18. Beside earlier press releases, see J. Margueron, "Quatre campagnes de fouilles à Emar (1972-1974): Un bilan provisoire," *Syria* 52 (1975) 53-85, Pl. V-VIII; D. Arnaud, "Les textes d'Emar et la chronologie de la fin du Bronze récent," *ibid.*, 87-92. More epigraphic material will be published in *AAS*.

19. See below.

20. LÚ.MEŠ *Ra-ab-ba-yu ša i-na e-bi-ir-tim i-na ma-a-at Ia-am-ḫa-ad*^{ki} *wa-aš-bu* "the Rabbeans who live on the other bank, in the land of Yamḫad," ARM I 6:9-11 (letter of Šamši-Adad to Yasmaḫ-Addu); cf. ARM IV 6:6; G. Dossin, "Benjaminites," 985; J.-R. Kupper, "Le recensement dans les lettres de Mari," *ap. Studia Mariana*, 108.

21. H. Lewy, "Šubat-Šamaš and Tuttul," *Or* 27 (1958) 60 restored the destination of these boats (ARM IV 6:21) as *a-na Ia-b[a-a]t-tim*^{ki} and considered this toponym a variant of *Abattum*. This restoration is epigraphically not very certain.

22. The name is spelled *A-ba-at-tum*^{ki} Inscr. Iaḫdun-Lim III:8 (var. *A-ba-tim*^{ki}); ARM 83:37; 84:14′; [*A*]*-ba-at-tum* Urbana Itinerary III:1; *A-ba-at-tum* Yale Itinerary 39 (see n. 23). H. Lewy's restoration [*A-ba*]*-at-tum* in ARM I 120:5 is not very probable because it would make Abattum a direct possession of Šamši-Adad's empire. In ARM VII 225:9, *A-ba-tim*$^{!}$ may equally well be read *A-ma-az*$^{!}$, cf. J. Bottéro, *ARMT* VII *ad. loc.* The name derives from Akkadian *abattum* "river gravel."

23. Urbana Itinerary, published by A. Goetze, "An Old Babylonian Itinerary," *JCS* 7 (1953) 51-72; Yale Itinerary, published by W. W. Hallo, "The Road to Emar," *JCS* 18 (1964) 57-88.

24. On the harbor of Tuttul see M. L. Burke, "Lettres de Numušda-nahrari et de trois autres correspondants à Idiniatum," *Syria* 41 (1964) 71, 91, 98.

25. As calculated by W. W. Hallo, "The Road to Emar," 72.

26. The identification of Tell Ṯadeyyēn with Tuttul by H. Lewy, "Šubat-Šamaš," 13-14, is based solely on the fancy etymology of the variant form *Tultul* as reduplication of Akkadian *tûlu* "breast."

27. E. Herzfeld *ap.* F. Sarre und E. Herzfeld, *Archäologische Reise im Euphrat- und Tigris-Gebiet*, I, Berlin 1911, 142. Insofar as I know, the mound has not been explored since then.

28. The el-Hneydah ruins, on which see A. Musil, *The Middle Euphrates*, New York 1927, 191, 220.

29. E. Herzfeld's identification of Tell Ṯadeyyēn with the famous Thapsacus of Cyrus the Younger's and Alexander's expeditions (*op. cit.*, 142-48) is totally unjustified.

30. ARM IV 6, quoted above; cf. J.-R. Kupper, *Nomades*, 55.

31. ARM I 6:6-13; cf. J.-R. Kupper, "Recensement," 108.

32. ARM I 24:rev. 2′, thus restored by J. M. Munn-Rankin, "Diplomacy in Western Asia in the Early Second Millennium B.C.," *Iraq* 18 (1956) 81 (following A. Finet, *ARMT* XV, 132). She also restores *ibid.*: rev. 12′ [LÚ *Ra-ab-ba-yu*] in the same position before LÚ Ḫa-aš-ši-im^{ki} LÚ *Ur-si-im*^{ki} *ù* L[Ú *K*]*ar-ka-mi-iš*$_{7}$^{ki} as in the lines 2′-3′. Prof. J. Bottéro kindly called my attention to the fact that from the point of view of grammar the restoration should rather be LÚ *Ra-ab-ba-*[*yi*], in genitive.

33. ARM VII 133:1-5.

34. ARM VII 165:15.

35. On an analogous overlapping of the terms *Sutû* and *Ḫapiru* cf. J.-R. Kupper, "Sutéens et *Ḫapiru*," *RA* 55 (1961) 197-200.

36. ARM IX 291:19.

37. ARM VIII 67:5; XIV 7:2′ (*Za-ar-ri-Aw-na-an*^{ki}); XIV 83:8 (*Za-ar-ri*^{ki} *Aw-na-an*). For the reading of PI in this ethnonym as *aw*, and the identity of *Awnanûm* and *Amnanûm*, see J.-R. Kupper, *Nomades*, 50, and I. J. Gelb, "WA = *aw*, *iw*, *uw* in Cuneiform Writing," *JNES* 20 (1961) 194-96.

38. Its eponymous ancestor, by whom the clansmen swore to observe and maintain a contract, was *A-wi-in* [*R*]*a-a*[*b*]*-bi*.

39. ARM VIII 11; see commentary by G. Boyer, *ARMT* VIII, 191-92.

40. *B.R. 513: Geographical Handbook Series: Syria* (Naval Intellingence Division 1943, reprinted 1944) 36; E. Wirth, *Syrien*, Darmstadt 1971, 429-35; A. Musil, *The Middle Euphrates*, 187-92, 197.

41. ARM XIV 83. Dadi-Ḫadun was probably the local ruler.

42. ARM XIV 84:rev. 12′-15′.

43. A. Musil, *The Middle Euphrates*, 188.

44. ARM IX 9:4-6 speaks of a considerable shipment of oil (over 20 hectoliters) which Nūr-Sin, Zimri-Lim's representative in Yamḫad, has sent from Alaḫtum; cf. M. Birot, *ARMT* IX, § 34.

45. Alaḫtum was the uppermost Mariote town on the Euphrates, it lay on the right bank of the river, thus providing for a complete control of both banks in that spot, it was a *maškānum* "depot" and a transshipment point, and it was a halting place for land caravans.

46. III:1; as noted by A. Goetze, "Itinerary," 60, "the sign marked x should be very narrow, i.e. preferably *a* or *za*." Variant spellings with or without *ḫ* are not uncommon in the Old Babylonian period.

47. The first items of the inbound leg in the Urbana Itinerary (end of col. II) are lost; then follow [*A*]*lattum, aḫ Puratti* ("bank of the Euphrates"), [*A*]*battum* (III:1-3). The end of the outbound leg in the Yale Itinerary has: *Abattum, aḫ Puratti, aḫ Puratti, ašar ša baḫra iziḫu* (enigmatic entry, on which see W. W. Hallo, "Road to Emar," §§ 60-1), *Imar libbi*.

48. R. Dussaud, *Topographie historique de la Syrie antique et médiévale*, Paris 1927, 454; A. Musil, *The Middle Euphrates*, 321-23.

49. It is hard to tell why it was necessary to make the 30 km. between Abattum and Alattum in two stages rather than in one; but there are other examples of very short stages in the Urbana and Yale Itineraries.

50. The affair of Alaḫtum is described in two letters to Zimri-Lim from Nūr-Sin, his representative at Ḫalab: A.1121, published in transliteration and translation by G. Dossin *ap.* A. Lods, "Une tablette inédite de Mari, intéressante pour l'histoire du prophétisme sémitique," *ap. Studies in Old Testament Prophecy, Presented to Theodore H. Robinson*, Edinborough 1950, 103-10 (English translation by W. L. Moran *ap. ANET*, 625); and A.2925, quoted in translation by G. Dossin, "Sur le prophétisme à Mari," *ap. XIVe Rencontre Assyriologique Internationale*, Paris 1966, 78.

51. ARM X 9:obv. 11-12.

52. W. L. Moran, "New Evidence From Mari on the History of Prophecy," *Biblica* 50 (1969) 50, No. 12, left *alaītum* untranslated; H. B. Huffmon, Prophecy in the Mari Letters," *BA* 31 (1968) 108, rendered it by "woman citizen," which makes little sense in this context.

53. Private communication.

54. This follows from the fact that, a generation later, the city of Irridi, between Carchemish and Ḫarrān, belonged to Yamḫad.

55. See M. L. Burke, article quoted in n. 24.

56. KBo I 1 rev. 18-9 = E. F. Weidner, *Politische Documente aus Kleinasien*, Leipzig 1923, 22-25. The name of the Mitannian prince has long been transliterated *Mattiwaza*, then *Kurtiwaza* (first by H. G. Güterbock, "The Deeds of Suppiluliuma," *JCS* 10 [1961] 121 n. 18). C. Zaccagnini showed case to read the name *Šattiwaz(z)a* in an article so entitled, *OrAnt* 13 (1974) 25-34.

57. The data of the Urbana and Yale Itineraries and of several Mari letters allow us to locate Aḫuna at Tell Samʿān, a large mound on the left bank of the Baliḫ, 30 km. from Tell Biyāʿ (Tuttul); see W. J. van Liere, "Capitals and Citadels of Bronze-Iron Age Syria," *AAS* 13 (1963) map 2 (without mention of the modern name of the site). Another town in the left-bank part of Aštata, according to the same treaty, was Terga, which is identical neither with the well-known Terqa on the right bank of the Euphrates much farther downstream, nor with the alleged Ṣerki of the Yale Itinerary (line 36), north of Tuttul, which was actually called *Ṣerdi*, see G. Dossin, "Le site de Tuttul-sur-Balīḫ," *RA* 68 (1974) 27. A third town in the same area was *I-gal-*[. . .], which, I believe, appears in the Emar tablet 75.18 as *I-kal-tá*, a town within the zone of domination of Carchemish, as was also Tuttul. I express here my sincere gratitude to Prof. Daniel Arnaud for providing me with information on toponyms contained in the Emar tablets and permitting me to use them in this paper.

58. See D. Arnaud, article quoted in n. 18.

59. The name is written ^{uru}*Aš-ta-te* in AT 89:3 and 172:8 (Alalaḫ Level IV, fifteenth century); KUR ^{uru}*Aš-ta-ti* in KBo I 6 obv. 21, 37 and KBo I 1 rev. 18; *Aš-ta-ta* (preceded by KUR or URU) elsewhere in imperial Hittite texts; ^{uru}*Aš-ta-ta* in the Emar tablet Msk 7219:11.

60. As mentioned in my "The Partition of the Confederacy of Mukiš-Nuḫašše-Nii by Šuppiluliuma," *Or* 38 (1969) 407 n. 3, the name may have survived into the Roman period in the Arameanized form *Athis, Attas,* or *Antas,* the first station on the Euphrates road southeast of Barbalissus (former Emar), now Dibsi Farağ. Recent excavations of that site showed that its settlement did not start before the first century A.D.; see R. P. Harper, "Excavations at Dibsi Faraj, Northern Syria, 1972-1974," *Dumbarton Oaks Papers* 29 (1975) 319-38, Pl. 1-14. However, a cuneiform tablet has been found in the washout of Dibsi Farağ, as R. P. Harper kindly told me; and a little farther east there is an unexplored archaeological site in which "deep cuts reveal mud brick walls on rubble foundations," according to M. L. van Loon, "The Tabqa Reservoir Survey 1964," *AAS* 17 (1967) 8, site No. 542.

61. KBo I 6 (principal text) and fragmentary duplicates KUB III 5 and 6 (E. Laroche, *CTH*, No. 75). Published in transliteration and translation by E. F. Weidner, *PDK*, 80-9 (text No. 6); investigated by A. Goetze, "Die historische Einleitung des Aleppo-Vertrages (KBo I, 6)," *MAOG* 4 (1928-1929) 59-66; commented upon by B. Landsberger, "Assyrische Königsliste und 'Dunkles Zeitalter'," *JCS* 8 (1954) 60-1. A new fragmentary version (BoFN 4475) has been published by H. Klengel, "Ein neues Fragment zur historischen Einleitung des Talmišarruma-Vertrages," *ZA* 56 (1964) 213-17.

62. H. Otten, *Die hethitischen historischen Quellen und die altorientalische Chronologie,* Mainz-Wiesbaden 1968. Otten's study met objections on the part of A. Goetze, "The Predecessors of Šuppiluliumaš and the Chronology of the Ancient Near East," *JCS* 22 (1968) 46-50, H. G. Güterbock, "The Predecessors of Šuppiluliuma Again," *JNES* 29 (1970) 73-7, and "Ḫattušili II Once More," *JCS* 25 (1973) 100-4, and A. Kammenhuber, "Die Vorgänger Šuppiluliumas I.," *Or* 39 (1970) 278-301. I have presented some additional points of support for Otten's thesis, from the point of view of North Syrian history, in "Ḫattušiliš, Ḫalab, and Ḫanigalbat," *JNES* 31 (1972) 102-9.

63. It has long been recognized, from the mentions of the land, or lands, of Nuḫašše in texts of the second millennium, that this region extended, roughly, from a line south of Aleppo to one north of Ḥama, and from the Orontes almost to the Euphrates, where it bordered on Aštata. The inscriptional evidence is conveniently assembled in H. Klengel, *Geschichte Syriens,* II, Berlin 1969, 18-32.

64. As thought, e.g., by M. Liverani, "Variazione climatiche e fluttuazioni demografiche nella storia siriana," *OrAnt* 7 (1968) 77-89.

65. This applies to the excavated sites of Tell Mardīḫ in the plain of Maṭḫ and Ḥabūbah Kabīrah on the Euphrates upstream from Emar.

66. Conveniently published, along with related fragments and duplicates of the so-called "Yarim-Lim Fragments," by C. Kühne, "Bemerkungen zu kürzlich edierten hethitischen Texten," *ZA* 62 (1972) 243-5.

67. Uršu was, very probably, located at the Citadel Mound of the present-day Gaziantep, as plausibly suggested by A. Archi, P. E. Pecorella, and Mirjo Salvini, *Gaziantep e la sua regione* (Incunabula Graeca XLVIII), Rome 1971, 45-6. It played an important role in the Syrian wars of Ḫattušiliš I.

68. Ebla has been definitely identified with Tell Mardiḫ by the epochal discovery there of vast cuneiform archives from the third millennium by the Italian Archaeological Mission.

69. As noted by E. Laroche, review of KUB XL, *OLZ* 66 (1971) 149-50.

70. Yarim-Lim was a dynastic name in Yamḫad and its appanage of Alalaḫ, to which Emar was originally attached.

71. B. Landsberger, "Assyrische Königsliste und 'Dunkles Zeitalter'," *JCS* 8 (1954) 65; accepted by H. Otten, *ap. Fischer Weltgeschichte,* 3, Frankfurt am Main 1966, 120, and P. Garelli, *Le Proche-Orient asiatique,* Paris 1969, 143.

72. Proclamation of Telepinuš § 12. Ḫurpana is otherwise unknown; if the enumeration follows from south to north, it would be located south of Carchemish, perhaps in the area of Manbiğ.

73. AT 89:3 and 172:9. The former tablet deals with slaves from the city of Aštate; the latter, a census list, remains unpublished as of this writing.

74. We follow the periodization and terminology of K. A. Kitchen, *Suppiluliuma and the Amarna Pharaohs,* Liverpool 1962, 3-4, 47-48. A. Goetze, *ap. CAH,* III^3 pt. 2, 13-20, applied the label "Second Syrian War" to what Kitchen called "First Syrian War," and that of "Hurrian War" to Kitchen's "Second Syrian War."

75. See n. 56. The old kingdom of Carchemish, conquered by the Hittites in the Second Syrian War, formed only a relatively small part of the new Greater Carchemish kingdom which Šuppiluliumaš created for his son Piyaššiliš (Šarri-Kušuḫ). The rest of it was formed from annexed territories in the eastern part of the Confederacy of Mukiš-Nuḫašše-Nii and adjacent states.

76. D. Arnaud, article quoted in n. 18.

77. Annals of Muršiliš II, extended version, ninth year, KBo IV 4 obv. II 58-68, published in transliteration and translation by A. Goetze, *Die Annalen des Muršiliš* (*MVAeG* 38), Leipzig 1933, 118-121. The Hittite king built a fortress above the city of Aštata.

78. KUB V 6 I 17-19 (*CTH* 570); cf. F. Sommer, *Die Aḫḫijavā-Urkunden*, Munich 1932, 276-77.

79. Msk 72.18:11.

80. Respectively, Msk 72.2:2 and 74.292; 72.3:1; 72.6:2; and 72.11:1.

81. KUB III 72 + KBo I 10 (*CTH* 172): translated by J. Friedrich, *Aus dem hethitischen Schrifttum* (*AO* 24/3), Leipzig 1925, 26-27, and A. L. Oppenheim, *Letters from Mesopotamia*, Chicago 1967, 139-46. Tuttul (^{uru}*Du-ud-du-ul*) KBo 10 I 42, may have been, as supposed by Oppenheim, the southern town of that name (Hīt), but more probably it refers here to the more famous Tuttul-on-the-Balīḫ, which was at that time the southeasternmost outpost of the Hittite Empire.

82. KBo I 14 (*CTH* 173); transliteration and translation by A. Goetze, *Kizzuwatna and the Problem of Hittite Geography*, New Haven 1940, 26-31; cf. *idem, Kleinasien*^{2}, Munich 1957, 102 n. 7, and E. Weidner, "Assyrien und Ḫanigalbat," *ap. Ugaritica VI*, Paris 1969, 525-26.

83. We intend to devote a separate short article to the Turira affair.

84. Thus calculated by D. Arnaud, quoted article, 88-9, on the basis of a broken loan contract dated in the second year of the Babylonian king Melišiḫu.

85. See E. Weidner, "Die Feldzüge und Bauten Tiglatpilesers I.," *AfO* 18 (1957-58) 344, 350; D. D. Luckenbill, *ARAB* I, §§ 239, 287, 292, 308, 320, 330; J.-R. Kupper, *Nomades*, 110-11.

86. It should be remembered that *Aḫlamû*, the ethnonym used to designate early Arameans, occurs as early as the Old Babylonian period. It seems that there was no real break between the West Semitic nomadic tribes of the early second millennium (which we often call Amorites) and the Aḫlamû-Arameans of the latter part of the same millennium.

87. It was supposed—notably by A. Musil, *The Middle Euphrates*, New York 1927, 210-22—that the Assyrian provincial center of Raṣappa was identical with classical Resapha, medieval and modern Ruṣāfa, 30 km. south of Sure (Sūrīyeh) on the segment of the Euphrates which interests us here. But the inscriptional evidence strongly favors the location of Raṣappa in the northeast of Mesopotamia; see E. Forrer, *Die Provinzeinteilung des assyrischen Reiches*, Leipzig 1921, 14-5; D. Oats, *Studies in the Ancient History of Northern Iraq*, London 1968, 55 n. 1. The Assyrian expeditions against Arab tribes took place much further south. Prof. J. Bottéro believed it worth while to mention that a similar toponym, ^{uru}*Ra(b)-ba-(a)-ia*, is attested in Elam at the time of Sennacherib (see S. Parpola, *Neo-Assyrian Toponyms*, Kevelaer/Neukirchen-Vluyn 1970, 289); this is certainly a mere onomastical coincidence.

88. More recently, W. J. Farrel, "A Revised Itinerary of the Route Followed by Cyrus the Younger through Syria, 401 B.C.," *JHS* 81 (1961) 153-5, proposed to locate Thapsacus at Carchemish (too far north), and G. Mendenhall, as summarized by R. P. Harper, quoted article (n. 60) 321 n. 4, at Jebel Khaled (too far south, cf. map, *ibid.* 320). My own investigation led me to the conclusion that Thapsacus of Cyrus the Younger and Alexander the Great was located opposite Til Barsib (Tell Aḫmar).

89. As evidenced by the chain of Macedonian colonies on the road from Zeugma (Belkis) to Nicephorium (Raqqa) via the Balīḫ Valley, which later became a segment of the Parthian Royal Road.

90. Strabo XVI:2:11. Quotations from Strabo are given in the translation by H. L. Jones in the Loeb Classical Library.

91. Strabo XVI:1:27.

92. Strabo, *l.c.*

93. Strabo XVI:1:28.

94. Plutarch, *Lucullus* 21; *idem, Pompey* 21; Pliny, *HN* VI:32 (142).

95. Cassius Dio XXVI:2:5; XL:20:1; XLVII:27:3-4.

96. *Alchaidamnus ho tōn Rhambaiōn basileus tōn entos tu Euphratu nomadōn.*

97. Strabo XVI:2:10.

98. Pliny, *HN* VII:16 (74).

99. C. Brockelmann, *Grundriss der vergleichenden Grammatik der semitischen Sprachen*, I, Berlin 1908, § 90; R. Ružička, *Konsonantische Dissimilation in den semitischen Sprachen*, Leipzig 1908, 109-19.

Publications of IIMAS
The International Institute for Mesopotamian Area Studies

PUBLICATIONS OF THE TERQA ARCHAEOLOGICAL PROJECT

Modular Preliminary Reports

TPR 1: G. BUCCELLATI and M. KELLY-BUCCELLATI
General Introduction and the Stratigraphic Record of the First Two Seasons,
Syro-Mesopotamian Studies 1/3 (1977).

TPR 2: G. BUCCELLATI
A Cuneiform Tablet from the Second Season, Syro-Mesopotamian Studies 1/4 (1977).

TPR 3: M. KELLY-BUCCELLATI and L. MOUNT-WILLIAMS
Object Typology of the Second Season (Excluding Vessels and Lithics),
Syro-Mesopotamian Studies 1/5 (1977).

TPR 4: M. KELLY-BUCCELLATI and W.R. SHELBY
Ceramic Vessel Typology of the First and Second Seasons, Syro-Mesopotamian Studies 1/6 (1977).

TPR 5: A. MAHMOUD
Die Industrie der islamischen Keramik aus der zweiten Season,
Syro-Mesopotamian Studies 2/5 (1978).

TPR 6: G. BUCCELLATI and M. KELLY-BUCCELLATI
Chronicle and Stratigraphic Record of the Third Season, Syro-Mesopotamian Studies 2/6 (1978).

TPR 7: O. ROUAULT
Les Documents épigraphiques de la troisième saison, Syro-Mesopotamian Studies 2/7 (1979).

TPR 8: L. MOUNT-WILLIAMS
Object Typology of the Third Season: The Third and Second Millennia,
Syro-Mesopotamian Studies 3/2 (1980).

TPR 9: E. GRIFFIN and W.R. SHELBY
Ceramic Vessel Typology of the Third Season. Forthcoming in Syro-Mesopotamian Studies.

TPR 10: G. BUCCELLATI with the collaboration of M. KELLY-BUCCELLATI and J. KNUDSTAD
The Fourth Season: Introduction and the Stratigraphic Record,
Bibliotheca Mesopotamica Vol. 10 (1979).

TPR 11: N.M. MAGALOUSIS, *et al.*
Sourcing Techniques for Ceramics and Soils, Syro-Mesopotamian Studies 3/4 (1980).

Final Reports

TFR – O. ROUAULT
L'Archive de Puzurum. Forthcoming in Bibliotheca Mesopotamica.

Audio-Visual Modules

G. BUCCELLATI and M. KELLY-BUCCELLATI, Editors; R. CLAYTON, Systems Director
The Joint Expedition to Terqa: The Second Season, Fall 1976, 123 slides, 25 min. cassette (1977).

G. BUCCELLATI, M. KELLY-BUCCELLATI and W.R. SHELBY
Terqa 1977, 125 slides, 25 min. cassette (1979).

G. BUCCELLATI and M. KELLY-BUCCELLATI
Terqa 1978, 123 slides, 25 min. cassette (1980).

Ancillary Reports

G. BUCCELLATI and M. KELLY-BUCCELLATI
IIMAS Field Encoding Manual (Non-Digital),
Aids and Research Tools in Ancient Near Eastern Studies Vol. 2 (1978).

SYRO-MESOPOTAMIAN STUDIES

A journal devoted to the study of the civilizations of ancient Iraq and Syria from late prehistory to the First Millennium B.C.—providing an outlet for the publication of primary sources and a forum for the archaeological, historical and linguistic analysis of pertinent phenomena.

Volume One

Articles by G. Buccellati, M. Kelly-Buccellati, L. Mount-Williams and W. R. Shelby.

Volume Two

Issue 1: M. C. Astour, *The Rabbeans: A Tribal Society on the Euphrates from Yaḫdun-Lim to Julius Caesar*, 12 pp.

Issue 2: P. Matthiae, *Preliminary Remarks on the Royal Palace of Ebla*, 20 pp., 8 plates.
Communiqué of the Italian Archaeological Mission to Syria Concerning the First Meeting of the International Committee for the Study of the Texts of Ebla, 2 pp.

Issue 3: P. Michalowski, *The Neo-Sumerian Silver Ring Texts*, 16 pp.

Issue 4: K. Toueir, *The Syrian Archaeological Expedition to Tell Al'Abd Zrejehey: Clay Figurines of the Third Millennium B.C.*, 15 pp., 20 plates.

Issue 5: A. Mahmoud, *Terqa Preliminary Reports, No. 5: Die Industrie der islamischen Keramik aus der zweiten Season*, 16 pp., 4 plates. In German.

Issue 6: G. Buccellati and M. Kelly-Buccellati, *Terqa Preliminary Reports, No. 6: The Third Season: Introduction and the Stratigraphic Record*, 36 pp., 14 plates.

Issue 7: O. Rouault, *Terqa Preliminary Reports, No. 7: Les documents épigraphiques de la troisième saison*, 12 pp., 4 plates. In French.

Volume Three

Issue 1: Ö. Tunca, *Catalogue des sceaux-cylindres d'Adana*, 28 pp., 15 plates (In French).
P. Amiet, *Review Article of BM 6*, 6 pp.

Issue 2: L. Mount-Williams, *Terqa Perliminary Reports, No. 8: Object Typology of the Third Season: The Third and Second Millennia*, 63 pp., 12 plates.

Issue 3: R. Tefnin, *Les niveaux supérieurs du Tell Abou Danné, Chantier A — 1977/78*, 58 pp., 11 plates. In French.

Issue 4: N. M. Magalousis, *et al.*, *Terqa Preliminary Reports, No. 11: Sourcing Techniques for Ceramics and Soils*, 32 pp.

Volume Four

Issue 1: J. Reade, *Mesopotamian Guidelines for Biblical Chronology*,

Issue 2: M.-H. Carre Gates, *Alalakh Levels VI and V: A Chronologic*

Issue 3: G. Buccellati, *The Descent of Inanna as a Ritual Journey to*
W. Heimpel, *A Catalog of Near Eastern Venus Deities*, 14 pp.